OVERCOMING DEPRESSION

A 40 DAY DEVOTIONAL

AUGUSTINE OPARA

Cover design by: Dr Opara Augustiine Chimrinma
Printed in the United States of America

GOD ALMIGHTY, THE GIVER OF LIFE AND HE WHO MAKES MEN, THE SALT OF THE EARTH

CONTENTS

Title Page

Copyright

Dedication

Introduction   1

Day 1: God wants you to be happy   3

Day 2: God wants you to be happy (2)   5

Day 3: God has Emotions too   7

Day 4: Understanding Your Emotions   9

Day 5: Another three things to know about   11
your emotions

Day 6: The Science Behind Your Emotions   13

Day 7: An Assurance from God.   15

Day 8: Analyzing your emotions   17

Day 9: A typical journal entry   19

Day 10: The parable of emotions   21

Day 11: Sustainable Happiness   23

Day 12: A foundation for Happiness in God's 25

word: Vision

Day 13: A Foundation for Happiness in God's Word: Sound health   27

Day 14: A foundation for Productive and satisfying work in God's word   29

Day 15: A Foundation for Happiness in God's Word: Meaningful Relationships   31

Day 16: A Foundation for Your Happiness in God's Word: Financial Stability   33

Day 17: Your Personalized Brand of Happiness   35

Day 18: A Guide to Your Brand of Happiness   37

Day 19: The Concept of Emotional Benefits and True Value   39

Day 20: An Empty Happiness   42

Day 21: Your Mind is Your Territory, Guard It.   45

Day 22: The Concept of Emotional Asymmetry   47

Day 23: Journaling to Take Control of Your Emotions   50

Day 24: Auditing your Journal   53

Day 25: Building an Emotional Map   55

Day 26: The Concept of Emotional Conditioning   57

Day 27: The Psychology of Champions   59

Day 28: Emotional Hygiene   62

Day 29: The Concept of Flooding   64

Day 30: Your Emotional Arsenal #1: The Word   66

of God

Day 31: The Emotional Benefits of Hearing God's Word   69

Day 32: Your Emotional Arsenal #2: Anointed Music   72

Day 33: Your Emotional Arsenal #3: Positive Memories   74

Day 34: Learning to forgive yourself   78

Day 35: Forgive Others   80

Day 36: A Lesson from Jesus about Forgiveness   82

Day 37: Dealing with negative emotions: why is it important?   85

Day 38: Dealing with Negative Thoughts: the Jesus formula   88

Day 39: The Jesus formula: dealing with Negative events and news updates.   91

Day 40: How to hear from God   94

40+1: Helping Others   96

40+2: Are you a Thermostat or a Thermometer?   98

40+3: Validation: The Greatest Human Emotional Need   100

40+4: God validates us in His Word   103

40+5: Are you willing to Reciprocate?   105

40+6: Your Joy is Under Attack   106

Prologue: 108

Appendix section: 111

CONCLUSION: 116

About The Author 119

Books By This Author 121

INTRODUCTION

I call myself the plastic surgeon God has blessed because God has indeed blessed me. A few years ago, I discovered that I was experiencing depression. At that moment I did not realize that it was depression. Still, I had experienced a series of negative stimuli and because I had not taken time to process each one the cumulative effect was a full-blown depression.

I want to share with you the steps I took to recover, including all the help I obtained from God. It is my prayer that you will be blessed by studying this material in Jesus' name.

To make the best of this book, I recommend the following:

1. Read one chapter a day and meditate on the lessons and how you can apply them to your own life.
2. Have a dedicated notebook with which to keep a record of your thoughts and carry out the assignments and tasks recommended on certain days
3. Study this devotional with a bible. We make frequent reference to the bible and you will be inspired to read more of the bible than has been referred to in this devotional.

I am certain that you will beat depression as I did; you will also help others to beat depression. Therefore be deliberate about your journey and keep records of your progress.

I would love to hear your testimony. You can e-mail me at: Chimrinma.opara@gmail.com

God bless you.

DAY 1: GOD WANTS YOU TO BE HAPPY

"Blessed is the man whom thou choosest, and causest to approach unto thee, that he may dwell in thy courts: we shall be satisfied with the goodness of thy house, even of thy holy temple"(Psalms 65:4)

If there is something I am certain about it is that God wants you to be happy. That is what is written in his word.

He has not only vocalized it but he has made adequate provision for you to enjoy the fullness of joy. By joy and happiness, I am not only referring to emotions but a state of emotional and mental well-being.

When I was experiencing depression, one verse of scripture that kept me going was Jeremiah chapter 29:11, I understood from that verse that God had a plan for me. That he was thinking about me, was more than enough reason to keep me going even in the most turbulent of days and darkest of nights. God loves you and desires to see you happy, anyone telling you otherwise is not saying the truth.

Assignment:

Look yourself in the mirror and say out loud: "God loves me and He wants me to be happy". Say it out loud as many times as it will take for you to begin feeling comfortable saying it to yourself.

DAY 2: GOD WANTS YOU TO BE HAPPY (2)

"Beloved, I wish above all things that thou mayest prosper and be in health, even as thy soul prospereth"

(3 John 1:2)

God has not only vocalized his desire to see you happy, but he has made adequate provision for you to enjoy sound mental health.

There are components to our emotional well-being that we shall be looking into later. For today, however, I would like to tell you that there are provisions for you to enjoy sound health, financial abundance, satisfying and productive work, and stable relationships all of which are vital to our overall happiness. It is time to discover what those provisions are and begin to appropriate every one of them.

Sometimes depression can make you doubt that God has your interest at heart. But I want to reassure you today, that I have been through depression myself and I know that all things are working together for your good, as long as you love God and are walking according to his purpose (Romans 8:28) Help has come, do not give up.

DAY 3: GOD HAS EMOTIONS TOO

I was pleasantly surprised to discover that God too has emotional experiences. And records of his emotional expressions are found at the very beginning.

If you follow the account of creation in Genesis chapter 1, you would observe that each time he completed the task for the day he took time to assess his work and declare that it was good.

One does not declare that something is good if one is not pleased and satisfied with it. To be happy and satisfied is an emotional experience.

On the other hand, in Genesis chapter 6 and verse 6, it is recorded there that God was grieved. That is another emotional experience.

The fact that we share this capacity to experience and express emotions with God is a testament to the fact that we are his children.

No earthly father would desire for his biological children to be unhappy. God is our example in the business of parenting; he loves you and desires to see you enjoy sound mental health.

Assignment

If you are familiar with the scriptures, this would be a good time for you to try and recall some instances where the bible has recorded emotional experiences and expressions from God.

Write them down and also write the passage where this emotion is expressed.

DAY 4: UNDERSTANDING YOUR EMOTIONS

To deal with depression, we must first understand our emotions. Here are three things to know and remember about your emotional experiences:

1. Experiencing emotions does not make you a weak person. There is a picture of what an emotionally strong person looks like and how emotionally strong people behave. Being aware of your emotional experiences puts you in a position to grow and become more productive.

2. Our emotional experiences are temporary. No matter how happy you are at this moment your emotional state can change if you are exposed to a negative stimulus. For example, suppose I were to gift you $100 and you are genuinely grateful. That emotional state would be altered if you were to lose $50 a few minutes later.

3. Every emotion you experience has a trigger or a stimulus. You might not be aware of

it yet but it is true. With emotions, the memory of a trigger is equally capable of producing that same emotion at that same intensity. Remembering a stimulus is like having that stimulus happen all over again in our emotional experiences.

Assignment

Close your eyes and attempt to call to memory any incident that triggered an emotional response (I prefer that you choose a happy memory).

How do you feel right now?

DAY 5: ANOTHER THREE THINGS TO KNOW ABOUT YOUR EMOTIONS

Another three things we need to know about our emotional experiences include:

1. Everywhere man is, there are emotional experiences. Even in the bible, they may not have been directly alluded to but man cannot be separated from his emotional experiences.

2. Your emotions will influence every aspect of your life, positively or negatively. It affects your relationships, work performance, financial decisions, and health. Your emotions are a vital part of your existence.

3. You are not at the mercy of your emotions. Your emotions should not determine the way you act and respond to situations. You can determine when to respond and how you want to respond.

If you are not sure then you could defer your expression of an emotional response.

I am not suggesting that you blunt or deny your emotions. What I am saying is that you acknowledge your emotions but choose to defer your expression of the emotions at that point in time.

Assignment

Call to memory any incident where you responded to an emotional stimulus immediately, and regretted it.

Supposing you had chosen to delay your response, would you have responded differently?

Write down how you would have responded.

DAY 6: THE SCIENCE BEHIND YOUR EMOTIONS

Your emotions are not arbitrary; they are a fundamental and inseparable part of human nature.

And yes there is a scientific explanation for the way you feel.

We understand from neuroscience that there is a part of the brain dedicated to emotional experiences, called the limbic system. While the part dedicated to logical reasoning is the neo-cortex. The emotional brain (limbic system) is older and faster than the logical brain and processes all stimuli before they are sent to the neocortex.

When we feel threatened, the limbic system takes control of the brain's blood supply and can inspire us to do actions that we would normally not do. For example, if a rabid dog were to start running towards you while you are reading this book you're likely to run and probably jump over any obstacle in your path, not to mention dropping the book. This flight-fight response is characteristic of the emotional brain once it perceives a threat. The emotional brain does not distinguish between a real threat and a perceived threat.

But the logical mind does. Each part of the brain has its functions which come with benefits and limitations. Skillful living is about mastering how to use the benefits while overcoming the limitations of each.

DAY 7: AN ASSURANCE FROM GOD.

When things are not going as we plan, the emotional experiences we have can lead us to doubt that God is interested in our well-being.

It happened to me, and I had to reason my way out of that negative thought.

When things are not going according to plan, it is usually that the enemies of our God are rallying for a fight. It does not mean that God has changed his mind or that he no longer loves you.

Secondly, they will turn around and lie by trying to pin the disappointment on God.

You will want to know how I got to know all this; I learned it from the account of Job.

The enemy went to God to accuse Job, and God was so confident in Job that he permitted the devil to have a go at him. God also set boundaries to those temptations.

God has you in mind; I encourage you to stay close

to him. An end to your emotional turmoil is here. I know because I experienced it. Your help is here in Jesus' name.

Note: take a step of faith and ask God to help you today.

Assignment

Read the first five chapters of the book of Job in the bible paying attention to emotional stimulus and the expression of the emotions of every character mentioned.

DAY 8: ANALYZING YOUR EMOTIONS

Sometime last week, I mentioned that every single emotion that you experience will have a trigger. Sometimes that trigger is just a memory. I also mentioned that memories are equally capable of triggering the exact emotion that the original event triggered with the same intensity.

Today we will take a step further, by learning to identify our emotions and the stimulus that has triggered them.

You will need an emotional journal for this exercise. I encourage you to write like no one else will get to read it, be brutally honest with yourself. Why is it important to keep records of your emotions and their triggers?

Because they serve as a way to stimulate your logical mind into being aware of how your emotional experiences are affecting you. Secondly, they will serve as data that you will put to use during your journey to recovery from any mental health issues that you might be experiencing.

Finally, by writing we activate the logical mind to process the situation and recover control of the mind from the limbic system.

Journaling will be so much fun once you become comfortable with it.

DAY 9: A TYPICAL JOURNAL ENTRY

I realize that this idea of journaling might be new to you, so I am going to offer you some help.

First, any notebook will serve its purpose. The information a typical journal entry provides includes:

1. Date
2. Time
3. What are you feeling at that moment?
4. Why are you feeling that way?
5. What did you do about it?
6. How do you feel about your response/expression of that emotion?
7. What could you have done differently?

In the beginning, this might feel awkward because it is new and you are not yet proficient at being acutely aware of your emotional experiences. But if you keep at it, you will get better and you will not feel so awkward when you begin to see the benefits.

The secret to mastering the art of journaling is to keep practicing. It will interest you to know that some chapters in the book of Psalms are very similar to entries in an emotional journal.

Assignment

Can you identify any verses in the Book of Psalms similar to entries in an emotional journal?

Note them in your journal

DAY 10: THE PARABLE OF EMOTIONS

Most times when Jesus was teaching, it is documented that he would use parables to illustrate and deepen the understanding of his listeners about the point that he was trying to make.

At the beginning of my journey with depression and journaling, I also struggled with trying to understand my emotions and how they influenced my life. I finally gained a peculiar insight when stumbled upon the mystery of parables.

Permit me to imitate Jesus and illustrate this with a parable.

Our emotions are like rechargeable batteries just like our mobile phones and computers work with batteries, so you and I need our emotions to function optimally and meet the demands of the activities in our lives daily.

Those gadgets function at their best when the battery is fully charged. Some functions will draw more energy from the battery than others. And we need to keep that battery charged to have the devices powered on and functional.

Our emotions power our everyday life. Even productive activities like cooking, shopping, and caring for our children and younger ones make a significant demand on our emotions. Negative stimuli make an even more significant demand.

It is wise to take time to charge the battery of your emotions every single day. Do not attempt to function today on yesterday's charge. Every day will require a fresh charge.

If you do attempt to run today on yesterday's charge, just like our gadgets will power down from low battery issues is the same way your mind will power down and you become irritable and frustrated. You can even get to the point where you cannot function optimally again. At this stage terrible decisions are a common outcome.

Sometimes all we need to deal with a lingering issue or a difficult task is just to charge our emotions to the point where our mind can deal with the additional demand of that task or issue.

This is where your time plays a vital role.

From today make time out to charge your emotions and watch the benefits overflow into every aspect of your life.

DAY 11: SUSTAINABLE HAPPINESS

During the dark days of my experience with depression, I tried several positive stimuli in an attempt to get back my joy and I discovered that certain things might make one happy but they offer only a temporary emotional value, with a more permanent regret. On the other hand, other stimuli will offer both short-term and long-term emotional value.

I discovered the meaning of empty, transient happiness through first-hand experience.

Some of those stimuli I recognized were sin but in my desperation, I crossed the line. Thank God that now I know better.

Some stimuli worked for me by producing longer-lasting and robust happiness like buying myself a few gifts and learning new things.

I bought an acoustic guitar and attempted to learn to play it, even though I did not make much progress with playing the guitar but the emotional benefit

I got from the experience was undeniably positive and it lasted for several weeks.

Even today, when I look at that guitar I still feel a sense of joy.

I have met many people who say that they just want to be happy, but have no idea what real happiness looks like.

After doing a bit of research I discovered that true and sustainable happiness is composed of the following:

- Sound health
- Stable and meaningful relationships
- Financial security/stability
- Productive and satisfying work
- Self-actualization

Imagine your happiness to be a round table delicately balanced on five legs. Each of these components listed above is an individual leg. We must endeavor to make investments in all five pillars. That is the only way our life will be balanced and our happiness and joy will be sustained in season and out of season.

DAY 12: A FOUNDATION FOR HAPPINESS IN GOD'S WORD: VISION

Where there is no vision, the people perish: but he that keepeth the law, happy is he. (Proverbs 29:18)

To perish in this context means to be robbed of honor and dignity. Conversely, when there is a vision, the people prosper and enjoy happiness.

Vision is essentially the unfolding of God's plan and purpose for our lives.

But how does your vision contribute to your happiness?

First, when you have an understanding of your vision, it inspires hope. It will help you to realize that despite the way you feel, and any negative stimulus around you. There is a brighter day ahead and the best is yet to come.

Secondly, a documented vision should be broken down into segments each with an actionable step and milestones. Each time your actions result in the attainment of a milestone, there is a joy that fills your heart. Similar to when we tick off items on our daily to-do list.

Your vision should be written out so that it will help you to maintain focus and keep working at it every day. My vision is to be "the plastic surgeon that God has blessed" and I am deliberate about positioning myself to be blessed by God and to be a blessing. This book is a testament to the fact that I am positioned to be a blessing today.

Your assignment today is to write your vision and make it plain. And if you do not have one, it is never too late to find out from God why he created you.

DAY 13: A FOUNDATION FOR HAPPINESS IN GOD'S WORD: SOUND HEALTH

Beloved, I wish above all things that thou mayest prosper and be in health, even as thy soul prospereth. (3 John 1:2)

My job as a surgeon gives me a unique perspective on life and a peek into the lives of lots of people, especially my clients.

For example, I have never encountered someone who responded with happiness when they were told that they had one form of health challenge or the other, no matter how minor that ailment was.

On the other hand, when I do have the privilege of giving a client a clean bill of health or discharging a satisfied client from my in-patient or outpatient services there is usually an unmistakable joy that they express.

Health has been described not just as the absence of sickness but as a total well-being involving physical, mental, emotional, social, financial, and spiritual well-being.

God has also expressed his desire to see us healthy. Not only that but he has made provision for everything that we need to enjoy sound health (2 Peter 1: 3&4)

What you need to start doing is to study God's word to uncover how to access the provisions that he has made for your healthy living.

Secondly, what is your idea of sound health?

Write down your response to that question.

DAY 14: A FOUNDATION FOR PRODUCTIVE AND SATISFYING WORK IN GOD'S WORD

Blessed is the man that walketh not in the counsel of the ungodly, nor standeth in the way of sinners, nor sitteth in the seat of the scornful. But his delight is in the law of the LORD; and in his law doth he meditate day and night. And he shall be like a tree planted by the rivers of water, that bringeth forth his fruit in his season; his leaf also shall not wither; and whatsoever he doeth shall prosper.

(Psalms 1:1-3)

This scripture found fulfillment in the life of Joseph, the son of Jacob. Everything he found to do, he did it diligently and it prospered in his hands.

Whether it was in Potiphar's house, in Prison, or the Palace Joseph's work prospered. I want to believe that he took pride in delivering excellent service and the compliments that he received in return served as a consolation for the betrayal he suffered at the hands of his brothers and his master's wife.

There is no higher compliment that one can receive from one's employer than to be given a raise or a promotion. Sometimes that promotion will come with more responsibility. Joseph enjoyed all of that.

Another example of how work influences our mental and emotional well-being is in the story of creation; God took time to appreciate the works of his hands at the end of each working day.

Work is an essential part of life, and even more importantly it is a vital component of your brand of happiness. But it has to be productive and emotionally rewarding.

It is time to personalize your work and be on the lookout for ways to make yourself more productive. It is easier when you have a vision statement, that way you can align your work towards the fulfillment of your vision. Remember that where you work today is a training ground and serves as a stepping stone to your next assignment. Therefore endeavor to be diligent in your current assignment.

DAY 15: A FOUNDATION FOR HAPPINESS IN GOD'S WORD: MEANINGFUL RELATIONSHIPS

'God setteth the solitary in families' (Psalms 68:6a)

Even though God relates with individuals, we see a pattern that throughout the scriptures, the relationships that man keeps have always been important to God.

Adam was given a help and companion with whom he could relate intelligently. In the above-quoted verse, God is taking the responsibility of setting solitary people in families. And he goes ahead to tell us the formula for maintaining such relationships.

He says "Love your neighbor as you love yourself". It is not a sin to love yourself. Loving yourself involves recognizing what love languages resonate better with you. By this self-discovery, you make it easier for people to love you.

How can you expect people to like you, if you do not even like yourself?

God also intends for us to relate with him. And the formula that works is: thou shall love the Lord your God with all of your heart, all of your soul, and your entire mind.

Assignment:

Make a list of three people with whom you currently have a strong relationship with or whom you desire to strengthen a bond.

Go ahead to note what steps you can begin to take to strengthen your relationship with them.

DAY 16: A FOUNDATION FOR YOUR HAPPINESS IN GOD'S WORD: FINANCIAL STABILITY

Many people believe that God is only interested in taking our money. But I can assure you that that is a big, fat lie from the pit of hell. Why would he have a prescription for people who possess the riches of this world if he did not expect any of his children to be rich?

Charge them that are rich in this world, that they are not highminded, nor trust in uncertain riches, but in the living God, who giveth us richly all things to enjoy; That they do good, that they are rich in good works, ready to distribute, willing to communicate; Laying up in store for themselves a good foundation against the time to come, that they may lay hold on eternal life. (1 Timothy 6:17 - 19)

God has outlined a pathway for us to enjoy financial abundance and a method that we are to deploy it: to be liberal and give in love using it to perform good works. He gives us a caveat that we do not trust in those riches.

Another reason that I believe God wants us to be rich is because if we do not control the wealth, wicked men will. I have seen how wicked men handle money, when it does not lead to their destruction they employ it in the pursuit of selfish goals and schemes to the detriment of most people around them and the society at large.

It is an error for money to be in the hands of the wicked because then the people will suffer. Moreover, it is part of the birthright that Jesus died to retrieve for us. I want you to say out loud to yourself: I AM RICH IN the name of Jesus!

The thing about financial stability is that it is not the amount of money or property that we currently possess that gives us stability. But rather it is the wisdom with which we manage what we have that gives us financial stability and abundance. If we go after wisdom like King Solomon did, money will come after that wisdom.

Go for financial education, and watch your financial situation stabilize.

DAY 17: YOUR PERSONALIZED BRAND OF HAPPINESS

God has many children, and each of us has our peculiar tastes and preferences. He is capable of making each of us happy, but I have come to understand that gifts are appreciated the most by people who realize the worth and value of such gifts, and then go ahead to ask for them.

A friend of mine was gifted a Parker pen by his wife on his birthday. Not knowing the value he left it on the table in the consultation room one day after a very demanding clinic session. As he was walking out, one of the nurses recognized that the pen was valuable.

She picked it up and followed him to return the pen. He was appreciative but concluded by saying that it was just a pen and that she should not have bothered.

She replied that it was obvious to her that he did not buy the pen by himself, to which he responded "Oh yes, it was a gift from my wife".

When he got home, he related the story to his wife and when she told him the monetary cost of the pen, he stopped using it to write altogether. Preferring to keep it in the case and admire it.

I share this story with us, to help us realize that your happiness needs to reflect your taste and your personal choices. In a way, your brand of happiness should be as unique as your fingerprint.

Your assignment today is to write down what the components of your brand of happiness look like.

DAY 18: A GUIDE TO YOUR BRAND OF HAPPINESS

I realized that this might be your first time carrying out this exercise.

So today I am going to offer you some help by showing you a sample of what your "vision for happiness" should look like:

1. Vision statement: To be the mechanic whom God has blessed (adapted from one of my mentors) your vision could be a verse of scriptures that you desire to have fulfilled in your life, or a testimony of someone's life that you desire.
2. Sound Health: I desire to live 85 years free of non-communicable diseases like diabetes, hypertension, and cancer
3. Satisfying work: I want to be able to mentor younger colleagues at work, enjoy the workspace interactions, and also deliver excellent services.

4. Relationships: I want to enjoy the fullness of my marriage, relationships with my children, members of my church, and community

5. Finances: I want to be able to give out a million dollars to charitable causes like the Smile Train, and afford a few luxuries like an annual vacation and a boat.

I will encourage you to take some time to document your own personal branded vision of happiness. It may take you a few days or weeks. Feel free to upgrade it at any time. And do not be afraid to dream big. Your vision for happiness is a living document that can be edited and upgraded at any point in time. Just remember that a living thing grows and not decreases, so if you must edit let it be an upgrade and not a downward adjustment.

Having written down your vision for happiness, the next step is to outline how you intend to arrive at each component. It will not be a bad idea to attach dates but do not be too ambitious. We tend to overestimate what we can do in 1 year and underestimate what we can do in five years. Focus on the actionable steps that will lead to the desired results and outcomes.

Finally, remember that each component should have a foundation in God's word that will serve as a prayer focus and inspire us to ask for God's help in the pursuit of that objective. Keep circling that desired outcome in prayer.

DAY 19: THE CONCEPT OF EMOTIONAL BENEFITS AND TRUE VALUE

Now that you have written down your vision for happiness, it is time to differentiate between valuable and non-valuable stimuli.

One surprising thing I observed when interacting with drug addicts and alcoholics is that the very substance and habits that they were seeking help to overcome can make them experience positive emotional states like confidence, excitement, elation, and satisfaction among other things.

In other words, the same satisfaction that you get from engaging in exercise, the drug-dependent individual can obtain it from popping a pill. We all know which of these stimuli poses more of a hazard to the health of the individual than a benefit.

Now suppose both the person engaging in exercise and the pill popper had the same goal concerning health, which is to live to 80, in sound health free of any ailments. Which one of the two is most likely to attain that objective?

In this context, exercise is a stimulus that adds value to that individual while popping a pill will no doubt make the pill popper temporarily elated but in the long run might be harmful. Exercise is therefore beneficial to health while popping pills is detrimental to health. Remember that they both produce the same emotional responses and therefore have similar emotional benefits but different true values.

It is the same principle in every other pillar of your vision; endeavor to make a list of stimuli that add real value to you and those that do not. For your happiness to be balanced, sustainable, long-lasting, and robust you need to be engaging more in activities and indulge in stimuli that add real value to you and not just those that give empty emotional benefits.

When a positive emotional stimulus adds value to you, it is a high-quality stimulus. When it does not add value to you it is a low-quality stimulus. When it takes away value it becomes a harmful stimulus.

Concerning health, let us analyze some stimuli

The stimulus has a positive emotional benefit	Stimulus adds true value	<u>High-quality stimulus</u> Example balanced diet
The stimulus has a positive emotional benefit	Stimulus does not add wholesome value	<u>Low-quality stimulus</u> Example fast food
The stimulus has a positive emotional benefit	Stimulus takes away true value from me	<u>Detrimental stimulus</u> Example sniffing cocaine

DAY 20:
AN EMPTY HAPPINESS

Ho, everyone that thirsteth, come ye to the waters, and he that hath no money; come ye, buy, and eat; yea, come, buy wine and milk without money and without price.

Wherefore do ye spend money for that which is not bread? and your labor for that which satisfieth not? hearken diligently unto me, and eat ye that which is good, and let your soul delight itself in fatness. Incline your ear, and come unto me: hear, and your soul shall live; and I will make an everlasting covenant with you, even the sure mercies of David. (Isaiah 55:1 - 3)

On the 5th of January, 2009 Germany was shocked by the headlines that its one-time 5th richest man with a net worth of 9.2 billion dollars had thrown himself under a moving train. He died at the age of 74 years.

I do not know much more about that incident, but the story gives the aura that the German Billionaire was experiencing empty happiness. Surely with a net worth of 9.2 billion dollars, he must have experienced some happy moments but none of those were enough to prevent him from committing suicide. It was an empty happiness. We know for certain that:

1. There are billions of people around the world today that would have gladly traded places with him wealth-wise
2. Most of these people assume that if they have access to even a tenth of the net worth (900 million dollars) they would be extremely happy.
3. Adolf Merkle had what most people on earth are desperately looking for today and yet ended up committing suicide.
4. Even in death, he was still richer than more than half of the people living in Germany at the time. And Germany happens to be one of the top-developed nations in the world.

With the kind of wealth, relationships, 'expensive toys' and experiences that he had access to I am certain that he enjoyed some level of positive emotional experiences. However, they were not enough to keep him satisfied. In other words, his life was full of what might be described as low-quality emotional stimuli. This would have resulted in an inner emptiness. A void, which many people are still experiencing today.

That void exists because something is missing; it is

called the Joy of salvation. And no matter how hard we try, it cannot be replaced with one million low-quality stimuli or even harmful positive stimuli.

The joy of salvation is a deep-seated satisfaction. A knowing that one's life holds more value than what we can see with the naked eye.

It is an assurance that everything is working out in your favor. The joy of salvation cannot be bought with money.

It is only God that gives that kind of satisfaction. I know because I have experienced it, not just as a promise, but as a personal experience with tangible proof.

I encourage you today to ask God, to give you that Joy of salvation.

NB: If you are yet to accept Jesus as your Lord and Savior this is the best time to do so. Just flip to the prayer of salvation attached in the appendix section and say that prayer before you flip to another page.

DAY 21: YOUR MIND IS YOUR TERRITORY, GUARD IT.

Keep thy heart with all diligence; for out of it are the issues of life. (Proverbs 4:23)

Your mind is like a garden of some sort. To be beautiful and productive you need high-quality seed (ideas) and fertile soil (sound state of mind).

In the parable of the sower, we are told that the word of God is the seed (Luke 8:11). Secondly the seed is sown in the hearts of men and the heart requires factors such as understanding, joy, patience, and ability to overcome offenses to produce fruit. (Matt 13:3-23, Mark 4:14-20, Luke 8:10-18)

I dare to say that you can choose which ideas to focus on. You might not be able to control which bird flies around a tree but you can determine which bird will build a nest in it.

Be proactive in determining the thoughts that dwell in your mind, and get rid of the unwanted thoughts. The logical mind deals with ideas.

With emotional intelligence, we can also be proactive about the emotional state of our minds. We can deal with negative stimuli and build a tide of positive emotions. The limbic system is the soil part of our minds. By taking control of the logical mind and choosing the thoughts that dwell therein, and practicing emotional intelligence which is spiritual soil management we can take full control of our minds and set ourselves on the path to being productive and joyful all the remaining days of our lives.

Assignment:

Study the parable of the sower in the verses of scripture that were outlined above

Make a list of the factors required in the heart before the planted word can yield a fruitful harvest.

DAY 22: THE CONCEPT OF EMOTIONAL ASYMMETRY

A study was conducted by psychologists on individuals who regularly kept a journal of their emotional experiences and they discovered that for the same magnitude of stimulus, the negative responses far outweighed the positive responses.

For example, supposing an individual receives a gift of one hundred dollars. The duration of happiness experienced was consistently shorter than if the same individual were to lose the same amount of money. I agree with this principle because I have observed even before I started studying emotional intelligence that when I lose a patient, I grieve for more days and even sometimes weeks than the duration I celebrate when I discharge a patient from plastic surgery services after having solved their issues. I hardly if ever recall any details by the following day.

This phenomenon plays out in every sphere of life. That is why bad news travels faster and wider than good news and stays on the headline sections for much longer the Russia-Ukraine war has lasted more than 2 years as of today and it is still making headline news and being actively discussed in many parts of the world.

Criticism will be remembered for much longer than the compliments we received on any given day.

An offense is more likely to be talked about than an act of kindness.

When a negative emotional stimulus is not dealt with early, the phenomenon of asymmetry predisposes us to take actions more spontaneously than if it were to have been a positive stimulus.

To overcome this asymmetry in emotional responses, we will have to consciously shift our focus from negative stimuli to positive ones.

We will have to turn down the magnitude of our responses to negative stimuli so that we are at liberty to respond more spontaneously to positive stimuli. It is something that we can determine in advance.

Recently, I was privileged to teach some youth at an international conference about anticipating negative stimuli and choosing not to be offended in advance. Later that evening, someone who heard me teach had her money and some other valuables stolen. But when she was sharing with me the story she was bubbling with joy. When I asked her how she was able to overcome the disappointment from that experience, she responded that she had chosen not to be offended even before the items were stolen.

Young people in Nigeria have a common saying that goes like this: this life is not balanced. When I remember the analogy of happiness delicately balanced on a five-legged stool I can relate to that saying. However I dare to add, that emotionally strong people will find a way to make it balance.

As an individual whose strength flows from your spirit, you can choose to alter the natural balance of your emotions and bring it to weigh in your favor.

DAY 23: JOURNALING TO TAKE CONTROL OF YOUR EMOTIONS

Earlier, we introduced the task of keeping a record of your emotional experiences and outlined the components of a typical entry.

If you have been consistent with your journaling, you would have observed certain things:

First, it is easier to journal on some days. And on other days it becomes an uphill task. To overcome this hurdle try to be consistent with the time you make an input. Try making your input for the day just before you go to bed.

Secondly, you would have observed that if you were sincere with the journaling, certain negative stimuli would have lost their strong influence on you. Conversely, you are now able to recognize more positive stimuli that you had been overlooking.

However, I want to introduce another dimension to your journaling. It is anticipatory journaling.

Now let me explain. Supposing you are a civil servant (like I am) and you can identify that on a particular day you are always upset. In your journal entries, you would have been able to identify at least one stimulus that upsets you. Advance journaling would be planning that day differently to have a better emotional experience.

In my situation, I perform elective surgeries every Friday in the hospital where I work. I am also a stickler for time and I observed that when time is not being used productively I flip a switch.

You can then imagine how I feel on Fridays when my elective surgeries start at noon, a whole four hours after I have arrived at the hospital. To describe me as irate would be an understatement. Initially, I used to sit in the lounge and binge on movies until I discovered from my journals the pattern.

I decided to plan my Fridays, scheduling a few activities that I enjoyed into the waiting time for surgeries to begin. On the first day that I executed that plan, I walked into the operating room, took a seat, and started reading. I had my Bose surround speaker playing some of my favorite songs too. By the time the first elective surgery started 5 hours later, I was halfway through the book I was reading and elated. It was so emotionally rewarding that it has become my habit ever since.

Another benefit is that the operation went very smoothly and the patient was calmer and more cooperative. Why wouldn't she be? She had good music playing and an emotionally buoyant surgical team that day.

DAY 24: AUDITING YOUR JOURNAL

Your journal entries serve as data. And data is of no use until it is processed and used to make necessary adjustments and decisions.

For your journal, that process is auditing. Make it a point of duty to audit it regularly. It can be every three days or once a week look through your journal and determine if you have any recognizable patterns. You will be surprised at what you will find.

Note things like

1. The most frequent positive emotional experiences you have had in the period you are auditing
2. What stimulus triggered them?
3. The most common negative experiences you have had
4. What triggered them?
5. Have you had any surprising encounters?

I know someone who discovered that her previously unexplained mood swings were closely related to her ovulatory cycle. Thus it was easy to make a diagnosis of menstrually related mood disorder and deal with it appropriately.

It was during the audit of my journal that I discovered that I love food. What I like most about food is the varied colors and the aroma even before tasting it.

I also rediscovered my love for cooking, because it reminded me of the hours I spent with my mother in the kitchen as a child. It seemed to be the only time that I had her attention to myself. I do not remember that we talked much but I do remember the tasks she assigned me, I remember getting to pre-taste meals and I remember getting extra portions of chicken. Thus was born and nurtured, my love for food and cooking.

Before I started journaling, my wife had dominated the kitchen but I wasted no time in scheduling those events back into my life. I can't say that I cook much at the moment, but when I do I take exceptional delight in it and I now cook more frequently than I used to do a few years ago. It is now a part of my brand of happiness, to cook and watch my family and friends eat with delight.

DAY 25: BUILDING AN EMOTIONAL MAP

The end point of auditing your journal should be to help you understand your emotional experiences and by doing so, you are better able to manage your emotions and motivate yourself.

The understanding of your emotions is an ongoing process and never really comes to an end. There are two simple steps required to build an emotional map. With an emotional map, it becomes easier to learn and grow emotionally. An emotional map puts your emotional growth and maturity in the speed lane.

The question then is: what is an emotional map and how does one go about building one?

To build an emotional map, you need to start by identifying the most common emotions that you experience.

Be sure to note both the negative and the positive

emotions.

The next step is to note 5 to ten stimuli that trigger each of these common emotions for you. You can tabulate them or just list them.

Congratulations, your map is complete. Now that you have a map, you need to start putting it to use. Before deploying your map go over it again to determine the nature of each stimulus to determine if it has both emotional benefits and true value.

DAY 26: THE CONCEPT OF EMOTIONAL CONDITIONING

And David was greatly distressed; for the people spake of stoning him, because the soul of all the people was grieved, every man for his sons and his daughters: but David encouraged himself in the LORD his God. (1 Samuel 30:6)

Air-conditioners have to be listed as one of the breakthroughs in the history of man. They enable us to live more comfortably in very hot and hostile climates. Imagine living in a place like Texas, Saudi Arabia, or even Sokoto without air conditioning!

In the same way, the temperature and humidity of our environment can be modified to suit us, our emotional environment can also be conditioned. In other words, it is within our capacity to influence how our environments turn out concerning emotions.

It is the hallmark of great leaders, that they can motivate themselves and the members of their teams to achieve feats, undertake tasks, and attain heights previously deemed impossible.

The other angle to it is that if the leaders are unable to motivate the team, the team will self-destruct. David had reasons to join the soldiers to mourn their losses, after all, he had lost family and a household in the very same raid where his generals and soldiers suffered losses and he was as human as they were.

But the bible records that he encouraged himself in the Lord, and by doing so motivated his men to take action that resulted in the recovery of all they had lost and more.

That ability to motivate yourself to deal with difficult situations, to give your best every day consistently, and to show up at work under the sun and in the rain is what I refer to as emotional conditioning. It is the secret of champions like Usain Bolt and Michael Phelps. It is the psychology of champions.

DAY 27: THE PSYCHOLOGY OF CHAMPIONS

I listened to a TED talk, which gave me insight into the way some sports legends motivate themselves to perform at their best and win.

Take Usain Bolt for example. Before any race that he participates in, he is often seen pacing back and forth, talking to himself. Those close enough to hear what he is saying, have reported that he often will voice out: 'I can do this' 'I am a champion' and similar self-motivational phrases. He is probably trying to drown the voice of anxiety (a negative emotion) that is ringing in his head by boosting his confidence and his performance. Champions recognize that they perform at their best while experiencing a positive mental state and mood.

Similarly, Michael Phelps the Olympic gold medalist in swimming has a different method; he will retreat to the corner of the poolside and plug his earphones while listening to a pre-selected playlist of some of his favorite songs.

Champions are confronted by the same stimulus that inspires thoughts of doubt and anxiety the same way the rest of us are, but they handle the stimulus differently. They choose not to dwell on the stimuli or live in the anxiety instead of dwelling on them.

They choose to replace those thoughts and negative stimuli with positive stimuli and focus on the positive stimulus until their mood improves. The positive stimuli serve the function of charging their emotional batteries and consequently, they can give their best consistently, every single time.

The difference between a champion and a regular competitor might just be the degree of motivation they have on the day that decisions are made on who becomes the champion. On that day that it matters the most, the champion delivers his best performance because his emotional battery is charged while the regular competitor is dealing with anxiety and performs with a depleted emotional battery.

You have a decision to make every single day; you do not have to wait for a moment when it matters the most to deliver your best performance.

You can be at your best of performances every single day every single time, if you would apply the psychology of champions, every single day.

There is a champion in you; you need a fully charged emotional battery to power it up.

DAY 28: EMOTIONAL HYGIENE

Then Pharaoh sent and called Joseph, and they brought him hastily out of the dungeon: and he shaved himself, and changed his raiment, and came in unto Pharaoh. (Genesis 41:14)

The day Joseph was sent to meet with Pharaoh, was a day he had prepared for, for a very long time. He already had a mental image of that day. This was why even though it is written that Joseph was sent for and brought hastily, he had enough leverage to ask for time to shave and put on some decent clothes.

It was a deliberate act to remove every negative stimulus serving as a barrier to remind him he was a prisoner fresh out of prison (among other benefits). When he appeared before the king, he looked like somebody worthy of the king's attention. He looked and smelled of royalty. That is why it was easy for the king to make him the prime minister after he spoke.

He was so motivated that he delivered an excellent performance. He interpreted Pharaoh's dream and went a step further to proffer a wisdom solution.

If you want to perform at your best consistently, you cannot afford to be careless about the management of your emotions (like I was). Do not let negative emotions linger for too long.

Be deliberate about eliminating negative stimuli from your space, and any negative stimulus you cannot eliminate, be sure to deal with the stimulus or process the emotion at the soonest opportunity.

Going by scriptural recommendations, it should not last overnight. (Be ye angry, and sin not: let not the sun go down upon your wrath: Ephesians 4:26)

DAY 29: THE CONCEPT OF FLOODING

The light of the body is the eye: if therefore thine eye be single, thy whole body shall be full of light. But if thine eye be evil, thy whole body shall be full of darkness. If therefore the light that is in thee be darkness, how great is that darkness! (Matthew 6:22 & 23)

During the Second World War, America needed spies who could speak fluent German, and that on very short notice. The options available were either to train ordinary people who could speak German fluently to become spies or to train spies to become fluent in the German language.

Eventually, they chose to train already active spies to speak German within weeks, instead of recruiting individuals who could speak fluent German and training them to become spies. It sounded a lot easier but how did they achieve it?

They used a technique called flooding. They

secluded the chosen spies in environments where they only communicated in German, read German books, watched German television programs, and listened to German radio. Everything in that space had to be in German or have a German influence and tone to it.

The outcome was outstanding because, in a matter of weeks, the spies who were learning the German language had become very proficient in speaking German.

That same principle of flooding can be applied to the management of your emotions, you can fill your space with positive stimuli that by the time you are stepping out of your room or your house you are fully charged with so much positivity that you can handle anything that comes your way that day. The higher the quality of emotional stimuli you choose, the longer and more robust the emotional buoyancy you will experience.

Assignment

If it is possible, create a space within your home or office that you can saturate with positive emotional stimulus. You can call it your happy place.

Make a list of the positive emotional stimuli that you can saturate that space with

DAY 30: YOUR EMOTIONAL ARSENAL #1: THE WORD OF GOD

And thou shalt remember all the way which the LORD thy God led thee these forty years in the wilderness, to humble thee, and to prove thee, to know what was in thine heart, whether thou wouldest keep his commandments, or no. And he humbled thee, and suffered thee to hunger, and fed thee with manna, which thou knewest not, neither did thy fathers know; that he might make thee know that man doth not live by bread only, but by every word that proceedeth out of the mouth of the LORD doth man live.

(Deuteronomy 8:2 & 3)

If you really desire to live, and not just exist then you ought to take advantage of God's word and put it to work in every aspect of your life, that is when you will experience true joy.

There is nothing else that has an all-round advantage in life like God's word. It is beneficial for our spiritual, mental, and physical growth and development. It is health for all our flesh

My son, attend to my words; incline thine ear unto my sayings. Let them not depart from thine eyes; keep them amid thine heart. For they are life unto those that find them and health to all their flesh.

Proverbs 4:20 – 22

By living, reference is not made to just breathing and moving around. That is merely existing

By living, the scripture refers to the capacity to exhibit God-like traits. Characters such as bringing hope to a dying world. Being able to encourage yourself and to encourage others amid tribulation. Being able to hold on to faith despite the negative happenings around us.

The word of God is a very powerful stimulus that can inspire and empower us to exhibit traits such as love, joy, peace, patience, gentleness, goodness, faith, Meekness, and temperance even while we are under stress.

The word of God can help us to consistently and unwaveringly stay on the path of good.

The word of God is an indispensable arsenal in our mental health toolbox. No matter how individualized your happiness and my happiness are, the word of God is the foundation for anything that will last long....including our happiness.

Remember your objective is to build sustainable happiness and not just happiness for the sake of happiness.

DAY 31: THE EMOTIONAL BENEFITS OF HEARING GOD'S WORD

I rejoice at thy word, as one that findeth great spoil.

(Psalms 119:162)

In addition to the value that the word of God gives us from the spiritual and logical perspectives, the word of God has emotional value.

Its logical value can be likened to seed which is putting it to use for doctrine, reproof, correction, and instruction in righteousness (2 Timothy 3:16),

The emotional benefit can be likened to soil management. No matter the quality of the seed sown, it must be combined with optimal soil management techniques for that seed to produce a bountiful harvest.

What then are the emotional benefits of hearing from God?

1. The word of God validates us. Validation is the most fundamental of human emotional needs. Some people seek it from other men; some people obtain it from themselves. But the most reliable and consistent validation that we can ever receive is from the word of God.

Then the word of the LORD came unto me, saying, before I formed thee in the belly I knew thee, and before thou camest forth out of the womb I sanctified thee, and I ordained thee a prophet unto the nations.

(Jeremiah 1:4 & 5)

2. The Word God inspires hope in the hearts of his children.

Remember the word unto thy servant, upon which thou hast caused me to hope. (Psalms 119:49)

The word of God gives us hope even in the darkest of our hours. When we meditate about God's promises and his very character, when we consider the testimonies of his previous interventions it is impossible to remain in despair. On one particular night, I was particularly feeling heavy so I reached out to play my selection of gospel music, and the anointed voice of a minstrel sifted through to me.....'He that walked on water holds my hand, why will I fear'…

Instantly I was motivated to keep pressing forward. Today that issue that was weighing me down is now a testimony. I was able to endure the hardship because of the hope and encouragement I got from listening to a song inspired by the word of God.

3. The final emotional benefit of hearing God's word we will be considering is that God's word inspires confidence.

If you read the account of Gideon's encounter with an angel in Judges chapter 6 vs 11 to chapter 8:23, you will see how Gideon was transformed from a timid farmer into a war hero simply by receiving a word of encouragement from God.

David also encouraged himself by hearing from God and having received confidence went after the raiding bands of the Amalekites to recover everything that had been stolen from them. (1 Samuel 30).

Assignment:

Read Judges Chapters 6, 7 and 8

Copy out and personalize the message of encouragement that God sent to Gideon through the angel.

DAY 32: YOUR EMOTIONAL ARSENAL #2: ANOINTED MUSIC

And it came to pass, when the evil spirit from God was upon Saul, that David took a harp, and played with his hand: so Saul was refreshed and was well, and the evil spirit departed from him. (1 Samuel 16:23)

Anointed music can serve as a very potent weapon against depression and other negative emotions. King Saul needed David to play on his harp, for him to be refreshed and the evil spirit then departed.

I have shared the testimony of how a phrase inspired from the scripture, served as a stimulus to boost my spirit on a certain day that I was feeling heavy.

Before I learned to play music in the operating room, I used to be grieved by the idle talk that went on among my fellow workers while surgeries were going on. I knew that I would achieve very little or nothing by asking them to be calm or avoid coarse jokes.

But playing anointed music has gotten many of them singing along with some of the anointed minstrels while we work diligently to save lives in the operating rooms.

It is such a beautiful sight, all thanks to anointed music.

Assignment:

In what space do you think that you could add anointed music to emotionally condition that environment?

Make a list of ten of your favorite anointed gospel songs, and make a playlist out of them.

DAY 33: YOUR EMOTIONAL ARSENAL #3: POSITIVE MEMORIES

We have heard with our ears, O God, our fathers have told us, what work thou didst in their days, in the times of old. How thou didst drive out the heathen with thy hand, and planted them; how thou didst afflict the people and cast them out. For they got not the land in possession by their sword, neither did their arm save them: but thy right hand, and thine arm, and the light of thy countenance, because thou hadst a favor unto them.

(Psalms 44:1 - 3)

Earlier, we had mentioned that memories are as strong a stimulus in producing an emotional response as the original event is. This fact is true both for positive emotions and negative emotions.

I believe this is the reason why God instructed Joshua to have a large stone brought out from the riverbed of the Jordan and keep them in a pile by the river after they had crossed on dry ground.

He wanted the pile of stones to serve as a trigger to remind them to talk about that testimony and to tell it to their children after them.

The testimonies of God's kindness to you should serve as a trigger to stimulate positive emotions. I have had such an encounter and I used it in the days I was going through depression. I would like to share it here to serve as inspiration to you:

After we got married, my wife and I used to go out to evangelize with the church team on Saturday mornings in Sokoto. On one such day, while I was getting the car set, I picked up the battery which I had charged overnight with a home charger.

I did not know that the acid in the battery was leaking. As I picked it up I felt a cool fluid flow unto my hands. I remembered the testimony that had been shared in the church of a brother who mistakenly drank acid and the Spirit of God neutralized (check the appendix section for details).

So I dropped the battery on the cemented floor outside my house and went to get water to clean the battery. As I poured the water in the cup over the battery, the acid got to the floor and started reacting with the cement giving off that putrid smell characteristic of sulphuric acid.

As I was still doubting if my hands had touched the acid or not, I looked at the black denim trousers that I was wearing and the acid had burnt a hole through the material.

It then dawned on me that God had wrought a mighty deliverance for me that morning. Supposing I had gotten acid burns on my fingers I doubt if I would have gone on to become a plastic surgeon. I doubt if I would have been able to work on this book because I type and write by myself. All these tasks require the delicate use of my fingers and hands.

On many nights I have recounted that deliverance and it spurred me on to give God thanks and praise. It has also helped me to hold on to God's word. Because I have a personal experience of the nature of the God I serve. He is dependable and always looking out for my good.

If he delivered me from acid burns, even before I realized that I was in danger I am certain that he has my interest at heart. And he is far better at working things out than I am.

From today, I encourage you to keep records of the good things happening in your life. They are all evidence that God is at work in your favor.

Assignment:

Read Joshua Chapter 4,

Take note of the souvenirs that God commanded be

brought up from the river bed and the reason why he commanded it.

What souvenirs can you begin to keep, that can serve as memories of victories and positive emotional encounters that God has wrought on your behalf?

DAY 34: LEARNING TO FORGIVE YOURSELF

And the second is like unto it, Thou shalt love thy neighbor as thyself. (Matthew 22:39)

One thing that I have learned from my emotional journal is that, when I set a goal or a task for myself and I do not meet the dateline that I planned, it makes me feel bad. That feeling frustrates me and paralyzes my mind so I do not even have the motivation to work on that task at all.

Say for example I had planned to wake up early to pray, and I woke up an hour later than I had planned. Instead of rising from the bed to redeem the time, I would remain in bed and scold myself for waking up late.

On a particular day, the Holy Ghost told me to forgive myself for my mistakes. I was surprised but I decided to follow his prompting.

I realized how empowering it is, to forgive myself and move on. Now even if I do wake up later than I planned, I forgive myself and smile. I start by thanking God for waking me in the first place and then I feel a surge of positive emotions which carry me through my morning routine.

It is emotionally empowering to forgive yourself. You should begin today, to forgive yourself for the mistakes you have made and the time you have wasted in pursuit of fruitless ventures. You are only human and to err is human.

Assignment

I would like you to take a moment and ponder, what do you need to forgive yourself for?

It might be for the role you played in a failed relationship.

It might be a bad decision that you took

It might be for an action you have taken for which you are regretting

Go ahead and write it down, then forgive yourself

Write yourself a forgiveness note.

DAY 35: FORGIVE OTHERS

And forgive us our debts, as we forgive our debtors. And lead us not into temptation, but deliver us from evil: For thine is the kingdom, and the power, and the glory, forever. Amen. For if ye forgive men their trespasses, your heavenly Father will also forgive you: But if ye forgive not men their trespasses, neither will your Father forgive your trespasses. (Matthew 6:12 - 15)

Living with Unforgiveness is a very detrimental situation for anyone. It is detrimental to our spiritual growth and our mental well-being. Anything that affects our spirits and our minds has in effect access to our physical body.

If someone has offended you and you are choosing not to forgive, it is like drinking poison and expecting the person who offended you to suffer the effects of that poison.

It gets more intriguing: you might have even decided to forgive however you have not completely done so. You will ask me, how can this thing be?

Recently I was counseling a young lady who had suffered serious emotional trauma in a past relationship. From her speech, I could tell that she had yet to forgive herself and her former lover. When I mentioned that she ought to forgive him, she immediately quipped that she had already done so and I believed her at that moment.

But when it got to the point where I was offering action steps for her to move forward with her life, and I mentioned that she needs to start praying for her former lover her response was why should I?

It dawned on both of us that even though she had made up her mind to forgive him, she had not forgiven him. Tomorrow I will be telling us about a lesson from Jesus about forgiveness.

DAY 36: A LESSON FROM JESUS ABOUT FORGIVENESS

Then said Jesus, Father, forgive them; for they know not what they do. And they parted his raiment and cast lots.

(Luke 23:34)

That phrase: 'forgive and forget' as biblical as it sounds does not occur in the bible. Not even once.

I have searched manually and I have also searched electronically and I did not find that phrase in the bible.

I am not saying that the principle of forgiving and forgetting was not preached by Jesus, it was. But there is what to forgive and what to forget, and who better to learn it from than Jesus himself?

While hanging on the cross, we see Jesus interceding for the soldiers who were doing the dirty work of crucifying him. If we have not gotten to the point of praying for those who have offended us then we have not truly forgiven them.

The second lesson is this: every offense committed comes with a penalty which can be considered a debt. In the human justice system that debt will only be paid when the law does catch up with the offender.

But no one can escape the court of heaven. That debt will surely be paid. When Jesus was asking God to forgive the soldiers, he was asking that their debt for killing an innocent man be forgiven them.

That debt is established in Numbers 35:31 and I quote:

'Moreover, ye shall take no satisfaction for the life of a murderer, which is guilty of death: but he shall be surely put to death'

Jesus was in essence asking the Father, to forgive the soldiers of the debt they had incurred by crucifying him.

How does this apply to you and me? Every time someone offends us, we expect an apology, restitution, or even a behavior change.

By choosing to forgive, we do not forget the experience but we decide to absolve them of the responsibility of restitution and an apology. In other words, we choose to cancel the debt that they owe us.

Jesus will never forget that he was crucified, and I am certain that if any of those soldiers make it to heaven he will recognize them. What he did was to absolve them completely of the debt they incurred by killing him. Forgiveness is very liberating. Without it, Jesus' sacrifice would not have been so impactful.

I am certain that you do not want to lose your place in destiny over Unforgiveness. Go ahead, forgive, and forget that debt you are owed by the person who offended you.

Assignment:

Is there someone that you need to forgive? To move forward with your life, take the following steps:

    a. Note down what the offense was
    b. Note down the debt which you think the person owes you. It might just be an apology, or something more complex
    c. Write a note to that person, acknowledging the hurt and also canceling the debt.

DAY 37: DEALING WITH NEGATIVE EMOTIONS: WHY IS IT IMPORTANT?

Be ye angry, and sin not: let not the sun go down upon your wrath: (Ephesians 4:26)

Today I will be sharing with you, three reasons why it is important to deal with negative emotions at the earliest possible time.

1. To avoid deterioration, when we do not deal with a negative emotional state the tendency for it to get worse is very real. Remember that we are wired naturally to demonstrate emotional asymmetry with a bias to negative emotions. Negative emotions tend to brew into a storm, much faster and easier than positive emotions. For example, disappointment can quickly turn to anger and irritability can turn to frustration in the blink of an eye. I

encourage you to ask for a minute if need be, and process that negative emotion before you take any actions or make any decisions that you will regret.

2. To avoid disconnection from God, in the account of the drama between Cain and Abel in Genesis chapter 4. After Cain's offering was rejected by God the bible records that he was disappointed, then upset and his countenance fell. God attempted the first counseling session with Cain, but Cain still went on to take action based on his anger and he ended up killing his brother. The consequence of that action was separation from God. Negative emotions will separate us from God and further complicate the original issue we were upset about.

In God's presence, there is fullness of Joy therefore I counsel you to do whatever it takes to remain connected to him by dealing with that negative emotion at the earliest possible opportunity.

3. By dealing with negative emotions early you would have essentially reduced the effect that the stimulus could have had on you. It is like turning down the volume on a radio set. The radio is still speaking but you cannot hear what is being said. Dealing with negative emotions early works the same way. Recently I was to perform a very

demanding and unrewarding surgery.

It was unrewarding because the condition that was being corrected by the surgery could have been prevented in the first place. It would require several hours of research from me; the operating time would be at least 8 hours standing in a poorly lit and even worse air-conditioned room. Finally, I would be operating with a new set of scrub nurses and residents as most of the more experienced ones had left the country for greener pastures.

But I was able to deal with that event in such a way that by the time I was through with the surgery even though I had an aching back and was emotionally and physically drained, I had this unmistakable satisfaction. One step I did take among others was that I determined from the beginning not to get upset. Secondly, I chose to turn that surgery into a learning experience for both myself and my residents. It turned out better than we had all anticipated it to turn out.

Assignment:

Call to mind any negative emotional experience that you have had in the past.

How would that event have turned out if you had handled it differently by emotionally conditioning that space?

DAY 38: DEALING WITH NEGATIVE THOUGHTS: THE JESUS FORMULA

And when the tempter came to him, he said, If thou be the Son of God, command that these stones be made bread. But he answered and said, It is written, Man shall not live by bread alone, but by every word that proceedeth out of the mouth of God. Then the devil taketh him up into the holy city, and setteth him on a pinnacle of the temple, And saith unto him, If thou be the Son of God, cast thyself down: for it is written, He shall give his angels charge concerning thee: and in their hands they shall bear thee up, lest at any time thou dash thy foot against a stone. Jesus said unto him, It is written again, Thou shalt not tempt the Lord thy God. Again, the devil taketh him up into an exceeding high mountain, and sheweth him all the kingdoms of the world, and the glory of them; And saith unto him, All these things will I give thee if thou wilt fall down and worship me. Then saith Jesus unto him, Get thee hence, Satan: for it is written, Thou shalt worship the Lord thy God, and him only shalt thou serve. Then the devil leaveth him, and, behold, angels came and ministered unto him. (Matthew 4:4 - 11)

Jesus during his earthly ministry also had to deal with negative thoughts. Let us look at the steps he took to overcome:

1. The need for validation. On two occasions the devil started by saying 'If you are the son of God' I believe that this was a question of validation. Jesus was so sure of whom he was and what the Word of God said about him that he did not need to make bread out of stone to prove that he was the son of God. Where do you get your validation from? As a child of God, your validation should primarily be from the word of God

2. Reason your way in the word of God. The statement that the devil threw at him in the second temptation was a half-truth. Jesus was able to deal with that thought by remembering the full truth and making his response based on the full truth that he knew. Little wonder he told us 'You shall know the truth and the truth shall make you free'. You need to know the truth for yourself, study the bible, and internalize as much of it as possible. It is your surest ally against negative thoughts.

3. Be deliberate about where you obtain help. By the third temptation, the enemy had realized that Jesus knew who he was and probably had an understanding of his assignment here on earth. He now tried to offer Jesus a shortcut to achieving his earthly ministry. Jesus did not reply that the devil was lying, which means that he did have control of the kingdoms at that time. Jesus rather reminded the devil of the true source of power and help.

When I was experiencing depression, every time I remembered the deliverance that God had done for me in the past I was assured that one day he would rescue me from the siege of depression. And thank God that he did. Always remember who it is that is helping you, he is never late, and he neither sleeps nor slumbers.

DAY 39: THE JESUS FORMULA: DEALING WITH NEGATIVE EVENTS AND NEWS UPDATES.

And his disciples came, and took up the body, and buried it, and went and told Jesus. When Jesus heard of it, he departed thence by ship into a desert place apart: and when the people had heard thereof, they followed him on foot out of the cities. And Jesus went forth, and saw a great multitude, and was moved with compassion toward them, and he healed their sick. And when he had sent the multitudes away, he went up into a mountain apart to pray: and when the evening came, he was there alone. (Matthew 14:12-14,23)

As long as we are living in this world, we will

be confronted with circumstances that will elicit negative emotions from us. If we attempt to shut down or blunt our response we stand the risk of losing a part of us and will no longer be able to demonstrate empathy.

So it is best to deal with these situations the way that Jesus modeled it. So what did Jesus do after receiving the news of the murder of his cousin John the Baptiste?

1. He separated himself. Immediately after receiving the news it is recorded that he separated himself. I believe that he wanted to process the emotions that followed what he had heard.

2. He invested in providing solutions to the problems of the people around him. This can be so emotionally demanding and yet rewarding. One of the reasons why I experienced depression was that I had lost a huge amount of money. An amount which would take me almost 60 months to pay back supposing I did not touch my income at the time. I mean if I remitted my total salary as I was paid monthly without removing a dime, it would take me 60 months to pay off that debt. However on a certain day, I was approached by a young man whose wife had just put to bed she had a set of twins, and because of the prevailing economic hardship in the country, he could

not afford baby formula to augment his wife's breast milk. The babies were crying and he stepped out to clear his head. He told me that he was not in the habit of begging but that he needed help. I was moved to purchase some baby food for him and I noted that I had this inner joy and sense of fulfillment. Even in my situation, I was able to show some kindness. That's what I think Jesus humanly felt when he fed that crowd.

3. Finally, when he was done solving everyone's problems he was able to retreat into the mountain to pray. No matter how dark the night is, do not hesitate to pray. Pray in season and pray out of season for in prayer we can deposit our little issues of concern into the mighty hands of the omnipotent God.

Assignment:

Outline the Jesus formula for dealing with negative thoughts and events.

Supposing you are confronted with a negative emotional stimulus in the future, how would you apply this formula?

DAY 40: HOW TO HEAR FROM GOD

Today marks the end of your 40-day journey to heal from depression or any mental health challenge that you started with.

I hope that it has been a worthwhile adventure for you. I would like to remind you that you are not fighting to win, but rather you are fighting to secure the victory that Jesus has already won in our favor.

Today I want to help you gain greater mastery of our 'chiefest' weapon in this battle, which is the word of God.

To hear from God reliably and consistently we need to take the following steps:

1. Be born again and remain so. When you get born again, you become a child of God and every child has natural access to the voice of his father as a birthright.
2. Read, study, and meditate on the word of God. The word of God is God's voice in print. Think of it as a letter that God has written to you personally. Just like this

book represents my thoughts and some selected teachings in print, God's word is his thoughts, accounts of his acts among men, and his instructions and promises to you and me in print. Approach it with that perspective and it will inspire confidence in you.

3. Ask for the help of the Holy Ghost. One part of the ministry of the Holy Ghost is to teach us from his word and to guide us into all truth. Without the help of the Holy Ghost, I would never have been able to recognize emotional intelligence as a skill being practiced in the scriptures and I would never have bothered to learn it and become so proficient at it. Ask for his help, he is always so willing to be of help to us.

I have included an additional five chapters as my gift to you. I want you to enjoy the mental soundness that God planned for you to enjoy and much more, for you to help others out of the pit of depression.

40+1: HELPING OTHERS

And the Lord said, Simon, Simon, behold, Satan hath desired to have you, that he may sift you as wheat: But I have prayed for thee, that thy faith fail not: and when thou art converted, strengthen thy brethren. (Luke 22:32)

One of the incentives and sources of encouragement that I have for writing this book, is that while I was going through the experiences I heard God's voice saying 'When thou art converted strengthen thine brethren'.

At that time I did not understand what he was talking about. I was allowed to share my testimony on two occasions and each time it generated so much interest in discussions. This helped me to understand that depression is a much bigger issue than I had previously thought it was.

Taking a cue from the scriptures, I saw where Joseph was looking out for the emotional well-being of his fellow prisoners and pointing them to God for solutions.

I have come to accept it as a covenant responsibility because it allows me to solve problems. Since then everywhere I am allowed to teach this subject, I am bombarded with requests for private audience and questioning sessions.

Helping others is also one way we can condition our environments by investing in the mental well-being of those around us so that they will be in a position to motivate and encourage us on the day of our adversity. Remember the scripture says, as iron sharpeneth iron, even so does a man sharpen the countenance of his friend. Be the iron that sharpens the countenance of your friends.

40+2: ARE YOU A THERMOSTAT OR A THERMOMETER?

Iron sharpeneth iron; so a man sharpeneth the countenance of his friend.

(Proverbs 27:17)

Now that you are mastering the skill of emotional intelligence, it is important to understand that the company you keep influences the moods and emotions that you will experience.

If you keep company with pessimistic people who are always complaining, your meetings are very likely to become pity parties at the end of which everyone leaves feeling depressed, frustrated, or hopeless.

But if you keep company with optimistic people, in every challenging situation they are always able to find some reason to keep hoping. Little wonder that optimistic individuals are more likely to bring solutions and answers of peace.

What if you were able to turn a pity party into a brainstorming session?

An individual who is happy when his companions are happy and sad when he joins a pity party is a thermometer, just reflecting the prevailing emotion in the group.

On the other hand, a thermostat can recognize the prevailing negative emotions and turn the tide around. The world needs more thermostats.

Being a thermostat will require that you can recognize the prevailing mood, and when the need arises turn the negative tide of emotions to a more positive one. It takes practice, but it is certainly worth it because it is far easier to maintain a positive mental disposition if your close associates are enjoying the same thing.

Another incentive is to help someone else manage their emotions.

40+3: VALIDATION: THE GREATEST HUMAN EMOTIONAL NEED

Before I formed thee in the belly I knew thee, and before thou camest forth out of the womb I sanctified thee, and I ordained thee a prophet unto the nations. (Jeremiah 1:5)

Our greatest emotional need as humans is the need for validation. We need to be encouraged. We need to be reminded that what we spend for and are being spent for is a worthwhile cause. We need to be reminded that we are handsome, beautiful, and acceptable.

There is no greater validation than to know that you

are not a mistake. You were created on purpose by a master strategist and he has a specific purpose for which each of us was created.

Even before we were conceived, God had a plan for each of us. Jeremiah 29:11 says that he knows the thoughts that he thinks towards us, thoughts of good and not of evil to give us hope and an expected end.

You can rest assured that God has you in mind. Nothing happens to you without his knowing.

Everything that has happened to you is for your good; it will be evident over time if and only if you keep pace with him.

Today's task:

Ask for grace to keep pace with God in every aspect of your life in Jesus' name, Amen.

40+4: GOD VALIDATES US IN HIS WORD

For I know the thoughts that I think toward you, saith the LORD, thoughts of peace, and not of evil, to give you an expected end. (Jeremiah 29:11)

The word of God is overflowing with statements of validation to us, from a loving, kind God.

The most precious validation of all was when he gave his only begotten son Jesus to die in our place on the cross.

There is no greater love that anyone can have, but to die for another person to enjoy freedom.

This is deep, sincere, and unalloyed love. To bleed for someone who has been pronounced guilty without expecting anything in return.

Words alone cannot express that magnitude of love. It is only the Holy Ghost that can help us to understand it.

Again and again, I have witnessed God's faithfulness

and love in my life and the lives of those around me. This is another reason I am confident. I have a little knowledge of the one whom I serve. He is a good God. He knows what we need and goes ahead to give it to us freely.

40+5: ARE YOU WILLING TO RECIPROCATE?

If ye love me, keep my commandments. (John 14:15)

Man will always be attracted to love. And being loved inspires us to love in return.

I constantly ask myself what I can do in return to please the God who has lavished so much care and attention on us. He has kind words for us, he has numerous gifts for us, he has made all things that we need available for us and he makes time to be with us, even though there are a billion and more other issues that require his attention. The least that we could do is to offer him back our love.

Loving back our Lord is summarized in that verse of scripture....if you love me, keep my commandments.

40+6: YOUR JOY IS UNDER ATTACK

Lest Satan should get an advantage of us: for we are not ignorant of his devices. (2 Corinthians 2:11)

Our joy of salvation is a vital aspect of our mental health that the enemy tries very hard to attack.

First, he attempts to trivialize our emotions, and then he makes it look like anyone expressing his or her emotions is weak. And then slowly and steadily our joy fizzles out like a dying flame.

Do not fall for that lie, God expresses emotions as we have seen and there is nothing weak about God.

Jesus expressed emotions during his earthly ministry and there is nothing weak about Jesus. The Holy Ghost too expresses emotions, and there is nothing weak about him either.

The reason many people fall for that trick is because they are walking in the flesh. And there is something attractive about strength, about victory and winning.

As strong as Goliath was physically, he was an

emotionally weak person. Emotional strength and emotional intelligence are part of the heritage for which Jesus went to the cross. If for anything I will not let the enemy take it from me. I will fight to keep my victory, it is mine. The joy of salvation is my birthright and I am not losing it. Not on my watch.

PROLOGUE:

When Jesus told his disciples about the things that would happen in the last days, I noted that there were a lot of negative stimuli there. Those stimuli include:

- Wars and rumors of wars
- Famine
- Pestilences
- Earthquakes
- Murder of the saints
- Affliction of the saints
- Hatred of the saints by the people of the world
- Betrayals
- Abounding iniquity

Jesus described it as the beginning of sorrows; he said that many will be offended and that the love of many will wax cold.

But he also encouraged us not to be troubled because he that endures till the end will be saved.

To be able to process all these negative stimuli and overcome the offenses, anxiety, fear, and frustration that will be thrown at us we need to be inoculated with the ability to maintain our mental and emotional well-being.

Just vaccines drastically reduced the number of children that died from the killer diseases of children; I believe that emotional intelligence will reduce the number of people falling prey to the wiles of the enemy. Emotional intelligence is a deliberate attempt to keep our minds occupied and productive until Jesus returns.

Emotional intelligence is a skill; there is the knowledge requirement and the practice requirement to become proficient at it.

Keep studying the subject and keep practicing. You will become an expert in no time.

APPENDIX SECTION:

*Appendix 1: Prayer
of Salvation*

Heavenly Father, I come to You in the name of Your Son Jesus Christ. You said in Your word that whosoever shall call upon the name of the Lord shall be saved (Romans 10:13).

Father, I am calling on Jesus right now. I believe He died on the cross for my sins that He was raised from the dead on the third day, and He is alive right now.

Lord Jesus, I am asking You now, come into my heart. Live Your life in me and through me. I repent of my sins and surrender myself totally and completely to You. Heavenly Father, by faith I now confess Jesus Christ as my new Lord and from this day forward, I dedicate my life to serving Him.

Appendix 2: Testimony of the Brother who drank acid mistakenly and miraculously escaped burns.

The testimony goes like this:

The testifier was a young man who worked in a laboratory section of his organization. He was planning for his wedding that was scheduled to take place in a few weeks.

On one of those days, he had been out of the office to make arrangements for the wedding and returned to the office very thirsty.

He went straight to the fridge and poured out some clear fluid from an unlabeled container, assuming that it was water. As he was gulping it down, his colleagues started to scream at him. They told him that what he was drinking was acid.

He refused to accept it as acid but insisted that it was water. To prove their point, they tested the fluid in his cup with litmus paper and it came out neutral just as water would.

However, when they tested the content from where the fluid was poured out, it was acidic.

His colleagues marveled at what was happening, but he knew that God had just worked a mighty deliverance in his favor.

Appendix 3: My Story

By the year 2010, I had been a senior registrar in plastic surgery for 2 and a half years and was due to sit for the part 2 professional examination to be certified as a plastic surgeon in the West African sub-region.

I attempted that four times before I eventually was successful; each attempt was followed by a brief period of depression which I thought was harmless at the time.

Having passed the exam and was appointed a consultant in my Alma matter (a much-cherished position), I proceeded to attempt to drown my sorrows in my work. Tragedy hit again when one of my patients, a six-year-old male whom we were treating for a parotid malignancy died.

Not long after, I lost a huge amount of money that was entrusted to me, and even if I were to repay that sum, it would take me more than thirty months to pay my whole salary and not take a dime out of it.

The multiple negative stimuli tilted me into a full-blown depression, and I made a series of bad decisions. My situation deteriorated and I saw myself becoming a recluse. If I was drawn out by any effort a monster manifested.

At a point, I started having ideas of suicide.

My breakthrough came when I read an article featured in the World Economic Forum blog, titled "Ten Things that Emotionally Strong People Do Not Do". I came across a key word emotional intelligence.

I took more interest and started researching, reading, and watching TED talks on emotional intelligence.

It was when I recognized it as a skill used in the bible by some prominent characters like Joseph, David, Artaxerxes, and Paul that it dawned on me that emotional intelligence was to mental health what vaccines are to infectious diseases.

As I gained mastery of the skill, the siege of depression lifted from my heart and my relationships began to improve on all fronts.

I have been invited to teach about emotional intelligence and mental health severally, and on each occasion, I am amazed at the number of people receiving answers of peace. I believe that you shall also receive an answer of peace in Jesus' name, Amen.

CONCLUSION:

I am certain that this book has been a blessing to you. I would love to hear your testimony.

For one it will make me glad.

Secondly, it will validate the work that we set out to do. which is to create a tool with which people going through a difficult time can find hope and healing.

You can give us feedback on the customer review section of the selar.co link where you made the purchase or write me an email: Chimrinma.opara@gmail.com

If you feel led to have us speak to your congregation, I will be most willing.

 I encourage you to get in touch with me at the most convenient time and let us get working on it already (smiles).

There are other materials that will help to aid your recovery to mental soundness. Do well to check them out.

Finally, your happiness, total health and mental soundness are important to me that is why i have shared my thought with you.

God bless you in Jesus name. Amen.

Opara Augustine Chimrinma

(The plastic surgeon whom God has helped)

ABOUT THE AUTHOR

Augustine Chimrinma Opara

Augustine Chimrinma opara is a plastic surgeon, counsellor and part time pastor with the living Faith church world wide

Beginning in the year 2010, he went through a series of life experiences that resulted in full blown depression by 2019.
By the help of the Holy Spirit he has fully recovered and has been inspired to share both his testimony and the steps that he took in order to help other people both to recover and avoid falling into the the trap of depression and mental health issues.

Augustine Chimrinma Opara, is a plastic surgeon, counselor, and part-time pastor with the Living Faith Church World Wide.

Beginning in the year 2010 he experienced a series of traumatizing events that resulted in full-blown depression by 2019.

With the help of the Holy Spirit, he has fully recovered and has been inspired to share both his testimony and the steps that he took to recover and avoid falling into the trap of depression and mental health issues.

BOOKS BY THIS AUTHOR

Beauty For Ashes: Developing An Emotional Strategy For A Successful And Fulfilled Life

I Believe God Is A Farmer

Gaining Momentum